MIDNIGHT MUSINGS

Saumya Yadav

To my friends Dhruvika, Shreya, Shalini, Divyaj, and Darpan!

Thank you

Content

1. Midnight Musings
2. Stillness of Time
3. Free Spirits
4. Night Sky
5. Sweet Summer Child
6. The Crossway
7. Snowflakes
8. One Day
9. Last Ounce
10. Alive or Dead
11. Together or Not?
12. Abyss
13. Living Backwards
14. A Young Girl
15. Holding on or Letting Go
16. Thousand Pieces
17. Tired
18. Memories
19. Adult or Child?
20. Summer Breeze or Thunderstorm?
21. My Glass Cubicle
22. Hear Me Now!
23. Hope
24. Confidence
25. Yearning and Wondering
26. Consistent
27. Eyes
28. Beauty of the Moments
29. Sands of Love
30. Home
31. Falling for You
32. Sky in the Night
33. Hostel Room
34. It will be over One Day
35. Wishes

36. Never Free!
37. Perhaps Because
38. Fly Away
39. Convenience
40. Keep Going
41. Our Invisible World
42. Evolution
43. Nurtured
44. Love, Acceptance and Validation
45. This world is too big for me!
46. Trapped
47. A Lifetime ago
48. Present or Absent?
49. Wish I was there with You
50. Ruins
51. Dearness to Dreadness
52. Maiden Road
53. Feelings
54. Irony
55. Greys

About the Author

Saumya is a research scientist currently working in a Pharma consultancy in Chennai. She holds a Ph.D. degree in the field of Biophysics from IIT Bombay. Originally, she is from Rae Bareli in Uttar Pradesh, an extension of Lucknow- a city that celebrates love, history and food. It is a testament of brewing modern lifestyle with the old one. This city epitomises beauty, grace and elegance. Poetries and '*shayaris*' are one of the cherished art forms of this city. Saumya's journey of inking her poetries started with her father's love for them. He has been an avid follower of poets like Ali Jawad Zaidi, Mansoor Ahmed, Agha Kashmiri, Anand Narain, Amir Meenai and many more. Although he has rooted for local writers most of his life, he follows many more poets (both old and new) too. Ramdhari Singh Dinkar ji being one of his all-time favorites, closely followed by Harivansh Rai Bacchan ji. Starting from reading his books in secret to finally being gifted her own, Saumya loved how much weight and beauty words can hold, especially those written in Urdu language. Her personal opinion is that Urdu is one of the best languages to write poetries and express emotions. Although she has read and written some poems in Hindi, writing beautiful verses in Urdu and touching people's lives is something she desires to achieve someday. The first book her father gifted Saumya was 'The Discovery of India', which is a compilation of letters Pandit Nehru wrote to his beloved daughter Indira from prison. His letters are a perfect example of confluence of his love for his daughter with his love for the country and its people.

Apart from her childhood experiences, Saumya was exposed to an ocean of contemporary and foreign authors by her dear friends during her college days. Shreya, her first roommate is a milestone figure in introducing her to thriller and mystery. Dhruvika on the other hand made Saumya see the magic of words and effect different writing styles can have on its reader. She also introduced Saumya to the richness of philosophy and Russian literature. While personal interests of Saumya helped her explore English authors, Veena introduced her to the works of French and Japanese authors. Darpan on the other hand, made her remember after all these years of reading foreign literature, her long-lost childhood love for hindi and urdu literature. The journey still goes on, but Saumya feels her interests now have a ground to spread their roots. She now understands that her love for writing is a reflection of her love for her father.

Among various forms of writing, poetries are Saumya's delight. She has been penning them down for some years now. At this stage she feels encouraged to take a step forward and compile some of her pieces into a book. While some of her poems are inspired by her friends and different people around her, her muse mostly remains her mother whom she loves dearly. This will be reflected in some pieces of this book.

Although never being confident enough about her work, Saumya wishes to publish a story book of her own one day. These are her humble beginnings.

1. Midnight Musings

To make sense of this wretchedness,
The constant vileness yet kindness
that I suffer from.
The darkness that sits heavy
in unexplored corners of my heart.
It takes every night to get past it,
and get through another day.
When the teachings of childhood
don't get a place in this world.
I feel lost!
To come in terms with
How things have turned out,
The constant hatred
that I am subjected to.
It all takes one night after the other.
But this complete sense of coming
to terms with it is biting me off.
This night takes a lot from me
yet gives me a space to get a hold on me.
I cannot complain,
As it is teaching me new ways
to breathe again.
I like this aloofness, but
I am afraid of this silence too.

I wish I had a 'happy place'
to come back to.
Some place or person,
that I could call 'home'.

2. Stillness of Time

I want to lie here with you
under the stars.
It does not matter if they are few
or too many,
if they are too hazy or too shiny.
I want to see the shadows
of moon in your eyes,
and feel alive,
while they touch me
with those shadows.
Listening to your breath
as my sleeping song,
I want to lie here
while the time goes along,
and silence become our words.
The words that we share
through the night.
Until morning comes
and the stars are all gone.

3. Free Spirits

Free spirits should never be held dearly.
For they will shake you,
while you enjoy that beautiful cursed ride.
You will be bound with the need to fly
with the cursed fate of freedom.
You will get hurt,
By your own efforts,
and feel weak, until
it all sets you free.
Then, you will learn to soar high,
and that curse will
take shape in your flight.

You will be alone and empty.
But don't look back!
Don't look back, because,
you will feel both jealousy and pity.
That innocence is no longer there,
and naivety is long gone.
There is no turning back now!
This freedom gave you wings,
but devoid you of your warmth.
You can't shred them now.
It runs in your veins and

there is no stop.
And with you, it goes on,
The ever-lonely free spirit,
and its free nomadic form!

4. Night Sky

This Night sky is so distant,
yet so close.
As if I can touch it,
with my bare hands, or
stroke it with my nose.
Like a silent lover,
whose eyes are all for me,
It gets me wondering
what is more beautiful?
Its darkness or its mystery!
Lying here, I am present
quite far from my head,
floating with slow breaths.
While the breeze
keeps touching my bare neck.
It demands me to fly along,
but this body cannot move.
Because I am up there,
among the stars,
wanting to be one.
Though I know I can't be!
But why can't I?
When we are made the same-
Clouds of ashes,

going down,
into the grains of stardust.
So, why do they belong to space
while I rust here on earth?

5. Sweet Summer Child

Every night has a different dark.
Which one is you?
Or do you think,
You are completely fair.
But I am sure that's not true.
Because tides hit the sea,
both in the day and night.
O creature of the shiny day!
You think your naivety,
and cheery eyes,
belong in the light, and you are
an element of good in the world.
But my sweet summer child,
I wish you were less mistaken
about your fate and innocence.
I pity your smile so bright.
Like me, one day
you will become a being in the dark.
It will grow on you and you will cherish
this grey, cloudy and cold sky.
When life would not be your friend,
but an enemy hitting you hard.

Waiting for you to stand again,
only to strike you back.
But savor your sugary present.
You deserve it!
The taste of its sweetness, and
the smell of its freedom,
will help you later
sail your boat to the other end!

6. The Crossway

Do you remember this crossway?
Right beside the street light
The one, where one evening,
you tried to surprise me,
and kiss me from behind.
But I caught you,
getting my cue
by your shadow in its orange hue.
Do you remember?
In the humid summer breeze,
the endless days that we walked,
to this spot- this crosswalk!
The ice-creams we ate,
which by the way melted,
because we were too busy in our talks.
We used to give it here
fresh stains before the old ones dried.
But now they are not there.
Vanished like my silent cries.
Now this crossway
Does not lead to your home.
And that street light is a silent zone.
I wonder if you packed them,

and took away with you.
Did you abandon this crossway?
The way you abandoned me?
I wonder if they will ever return
To unite with me.
And although I don't want to,
but I am waiting for them,
and you.
I wonder, sitting on this tattered bench,
if you had any questions too?
Do you long for me?
The way I long for you!
I wonder looking at the spring leaves,
how many more seasons
do I have to wait for you?

7. Snowflakes

O my beloved of mountains!
Leave your home, and be free.
Have courage and come with me.
Come, let us take this trail
covered in snow.
In the chilly winter night,
walk down these paths
out of our plight.
Come with me.
Let us tread, trip and fall.
Turn our miseries into glee,
but some of them, not all.
For that is beauty
of our paths together,
like slow and silent snowfall.
Come let us make wishes and pray.
They might take the shape of snowflakes.
Pretty in the moonlight, and
sparkling during the day.
By tomorrow dawn, we will be gone.
But they will reign as our remains.
Until they vanish too,
and the winds quietly change.

8. One Day

One day!
One day it is,
We all wait for.
Like a movie scene
We picture it the place,
where we are happy, and
have everything.
Going from rags to riches,
feeling the world at top.
Having the love of your life,
and that perfect job.
Giving best things to parents,
and what not?
It makes every bit of it
seem possible.
When reality is really,
far from it.
Making us yearn for it- One day!
As if that is all it takes,
The difference of one day.
Although it is not true,
But I wish it to.
At least I would have peace,

knowing the ladder between
my desires and reality is ONE DAY!
Be is full of sufferings,
or delightful.

9. Last Ounce

Flickering of a burnt-out candle,
beating of a dying heart,
last ounces of breaths,
from the chest of a dying body,
'Orange' of the sky
while the sun goes down,
and a departing soul.
What do you think is their world view?
And what is their state?
Are they here?
or have they already left?
Are they fighting to stay back?
Or to abandon and depart?
Is their demeanor desperate?
Like a magician,
putting forward his best tricks
in the finality of his show.
They reiterate the very purpose,
they are about to abandon.
The confluence of tragedy and beauty
reflecting best,
in their vanishing existence.

10. Alive or Dead

Am I really living?
Or just surviving?
Trying to defy the obvious
My problems- one day at a time?
My past has passed
and future is tucked away.
My present is present,
though mostly in my head.
I am alive and breathing,
but is that all for living?
Like a shape shifter,
I juggle between my heart and mind.
Though emotions are not dead.
But trapped in my head,
they sound like a meaningless rhyme.
While I question myself
am I really living?
Or just surviving,
one moment at a time?

11. Together or Not?

They say,
you do, what you do.
I do what I got to do.
Do not wait up!
We might meet
somewhere in between,
and go our separate ways.
Or it might so happen,
that we might not meet at all.
But remember this!
There is a place,
where we are together.
No matter what,
that is my place of being, and
that is where I belong.
Our world beyond,
all kinds of rights and wrong.

12. Abyss

Off I go,

into the abyss.

Like a leaf,

blown into the wind.

A nest abandoned in the end.

My time is done, and days are gone.

Served my purpose though,

and there is no grudge.

Bygones are bygone.

So it's time,

to hit the road.

13. Living Backwards

Does it ever cross your mind?
What if we are living
backwards in time?
What if our death
is the moment of our birth.
Maybe that death bed,
that accident, fall from the cliff,
that earthquake,
occurred to give us life?
Instead of taking it!
Isn't it why they say
that dying people can see clear-
of both the worlds,
the past and the future.
Maybe it is that state of transition
when they have not forsaken
their current form or,
adapted the new life born.
Which is why,
they could see everything-
our life backwards,
and forward moving time.

14. A Young Girl

What does a young girl like me
know about love?
Intricacies of its miracle
are beyond me.
Though I understand
the desires that linger,
in the darkness of a heart.
The desire to consume and own.
Own and damage,
a being with lust and love.
This torn and wretched soul
has a long way to go,
before it beholds
affection in its stead.
To stop wandering,
I wander like a bird.
An unfamiliar nomad,
roaming the streets
of this familiar world.
Love might one day
cross paths with me.
It might want to
settle with me.
But it might be too late,

as I might be tired or
I might be dead.

15. Holding on or Letting Go

Holding on to life,
its ups and downs,
take a lot of courage.
But so does, letting go.
People who chose to live,
are taken to be strong.
But it is a different story
on the other side of the coin.
It says they were too scared
to forsake their breath.
I have been on the edge myself,
but could not take that step.
It struck me that only they chose death,
for whom, there is nothing left.
The end of never-ending miseries,
a haunted tunnel, they fearfully trudge.
There are no diversions,
So they become a ghost,
to escape these ghosts!
While rest of us
find other ways
out of our miseries.

Using family, laugh and love,
mountains and beaches,
dance and songs.
We continue to live on.
Justify being alive,
while life being indifferent,
silently goes on.

16. Thousand Pieces

Why do I dream
to live an extra-ordinary life.
Yet have desires of an ordinary person
timid and trifling.
Mirage of love constantly flashing
in my eyes.
It keeps repeating in my ears
like a sermon in disguise.
Like I am a bird of hills
covered in flowers,
fruits and land mines.
Beautiful yet inaccessible.
In its world, I soar high
with smell of air and sky.
But there is no ground
to my reality.
I know that as soon as I land,
my flight will cease, and
I will be blown apart
in thousand pieces.

17. Tired

I gaze at the ceiling,
while it rains outside.
Listening to it-
the quite of every side.
And I realise,
how it is not the silence
before the storm.
But the one that follows it after.
And I am too slow to catch
what has transpired?
As I see my whole life
flash backwards,
in canvas of my eyes.
Not a tear, not a word
But suddenly I felt tired.
Tired enough to feel nothing,
tired enough to sleep.
So, in my bed,
I slept for a long long time.

18. Memories

Caught between remembrances
and urge to live in the moment,
I journey through the day.
Sun still shines these paths,
that I used to walk on
with friends and loved ones.
While I am still here,
they are gone.
The laughs we shared,
the cries that made us heavy,
kisses that made us fly,
and the hugs that kept us warm.
All are lost in time.
I wish these trees
keep their smell intact,
and become witnesses to our memories.
So that when we come back,
those days will be regained back
through their memory sac.
But for now, I am fine with
walking these paths alone.
These weary leaves remind me
of our laughing faces.

Happy or sad, I still smile
at the thought of you.
And just like that,
I keep taking these endless walks.
Waiting for the day, when
I will also not be around.

19. Adult or Child?

It's funny that
I see a child in the mirror, while
everyone wants me to adult-up.
To be one of them.
While all they do is agonizing and
mean things to each other.
They admire you in one moment,
and castrate your character in the other.
The innocence of a person
is taken to be fake.
For them, putting down others
is a piece of cake.

They want you to be good
But not good enough,
to make them jealous.
They want you to
find someone you love.
But not as good as
their beloved dove.
If being adult is
miserable and unsettling,
then I am happy being
the uninvited one,

left out of this party!
Because my mom taught me
to love and respect
instead of being crafty.
I ought to live away from their dark.
So, it is unsettling to walk
these paths of regress.
They call this 'annoying' and 'innocent',
Traits too stupid
for their grown-up world.
The reason is their jealousy,
because I can sleep
without a stone,
weighing on my chest.
I am unfriendly to their ways.
Free of guilt and darkness,
a child I am, come what may.

20. Summer Breeze or Thunderstorm?

Does it ever occur to you?
You could be
in a very dark place.
Your pathetic insides know
you want to be loved,
and cherished so passionately
and vividly,
that it takes away your breath away.
It engulfs you,
like an ocean does to a river.
You hope to lose yourself,
and die a thousand deaths for it.
But now when love is here,
at your door,
with all its perks,
knocking like a summer breeze.
You can't help but look away.
To you it feels like a storm,
from which you want to remain safe

You are not ready to face it.
Fearful to give yourself away,
You want it to go,
while it wants to stay.
So, you sit silently,
curled up at the far corners
of your bed.
Gazing through these sheets
at your window, and wait!
Wait for it to leave.
So that you feel safe from its pain,
and breathe your life again.

21. My Glass Cubicle

Yesterday I saw a dream
A dream, that we are at
the end of time.
The judgement day has arrived.
It's all blurred, but I remember
to have seen the most beautiful things
before I died.
First it was all in the air,
then it was ashes,
then it was clear blue sky.
After which came the water,
engulfing me in waves, hitting
my glass cubicle.
Oh yeah!
My glass cubicle, floating in water.
This Euphoria made me forget
the debacle I am in.
The death that I am about to embrace.
Maybe it is the best way to go.
Witnessing all at once,
then nothing at all.
Then it was all black,
and I was in space.
Like a pinnacle,

my cubicle hanging above the Earth!
Mama calls me out,
says we are reborn,
and are going back.
There's Papa and Chhotu too.
So, we start our expedition to
earth, its gravity and clouds.
Floating along them,
we see the misty fur balls.
Greeting us on our way down.
Then we fall fast,
suspended in the air.
With mountains and birds around.
I pull the hatch,
and finally land on the ground.
We witness the most clear
skies, lands and clouds
and not a trace of chaos around.

22. Hear Me Now!

Hey! —Are you alone now?
Do you hear my sound?
I have been talking to you,
gawking at you,
Waiting for your attention!
In your chest, I am bound
with your chaos-
the voice of inbound.
I am the silence of your sound.
The sound of your heart beating,
the sound of your pen writing.

Do you hear me?
I am the sound of your breathing,
Breeze flowing,
and night growing on you.
Feel my presence,
rumbling through your ears.
Quietly whispering-
'Don't worry, you are not alone,
We are all lonely together here.'
I have been here before you
and I will be here after you.
I am the present to your future

and future to your past.
You are no more than a combination
of different perceptions,
until one of it translates into your existence.
Your matter is anti-matter
to other perceptions.
Those perceptions are your realities
in the parallel world.
So, you are only an illusion,
until you are perceived.
"You" exist, but only in visions.
Your matters and anti-matters run
in opposite direction.
But gravitate to each other
and converge in 'you'.
So, tell me now, do you hear it?
The voice of your chaos? It's me.
Repeating itself, since time immemorial.
Recognize me, as I am your home.
The voice of your chaos,
and arcade of life
between your birth and burial.

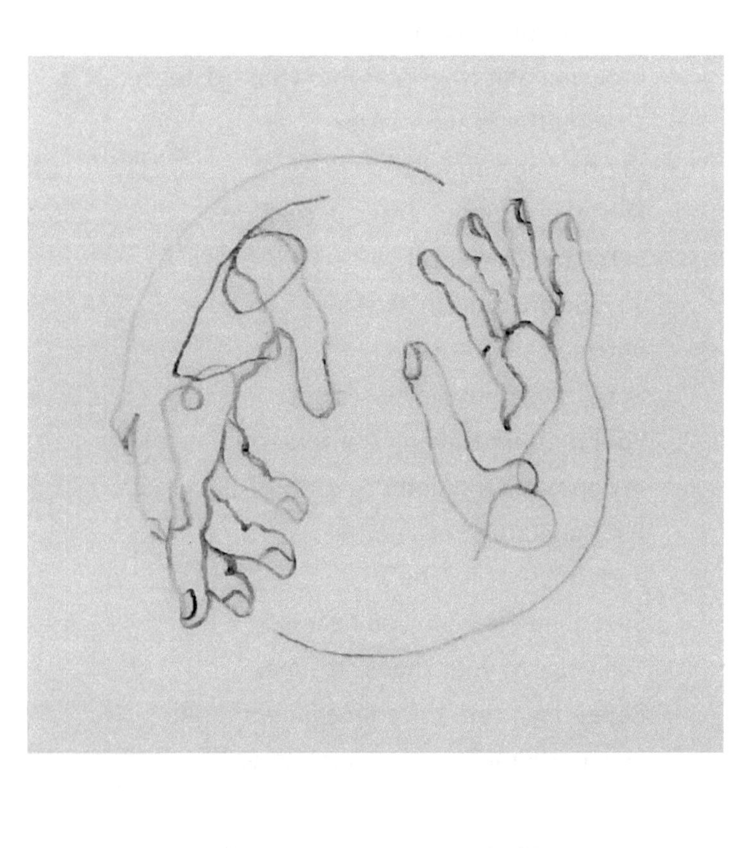

23. Hope

Let us again delve deep
in this night-
the never-ending ridge of possibilities.
And fill our canvas with hope.
Hope, that anything is possible
while we have our eyes closed.
And dream,
dream like a child,
under this clear moonlit sky.
And fly,
fly like a bird,
with the winds
under this canopy of stars.
To a world where your dreams belong,
and your soul sings you
melodious songs.
Where you are not
a careful existence,
but a carefree bird.

24. Confidence

Feeling of confidence
Soars high into over-confidence
In a minute, too high to handle
And with a slightest prick
It goes back to ashes
Dwindling like a burnt-out candle

25. Yearning and Wondering

Sometimes, I play like a fire,
with my insides burning.
But sometimes this soul lazes it off,
refusing to even inspire.
Life is a menace.
Some say it's a race,
fast to catch up.
It must be walked with
patience and grace.
But I cannot seem to
turn to it and embrace,
it's never ending, one-sided game.

Lessons of good and bad
fair and just,
that I learned when I was little,
are enclosed in a case,
beside the child I used to be.
Making me wonder if they were true
or was it just a phase
Like my present days.
When the old age comes,

there will be new lessons
to learn,
starting from the base.

26. Consistent

In these sufferings
I have grown,
grown away,
and distant from you.
You are so consistent
in showering me
with disappointment,
that I am not sure,
If I should be sad,
or if I should be content?

27. Eyes

Look in their eyes.
They never lie.
Lips might say,
a thousand different things.
But expressions never lie.
They are witness to their truths
only if you know,
how to look in their eyes?
Lips can be beautiful,
but eyes are alive.
Door to their silent frustrations,
revolts and desires,
they are a tunnel
hidden behind their tranquil smile.
They behold the darkest secrets,
and gates to their soul.
Speak their own language,
one that is free of delude.
So, read their eyes
while they are busy living
their routine mundane lies.

28. Beauty of the Moments

People are lovely
What they do is not.
Moments are beautiful,
Life is not.
I guess that is why they say-
Life is a film,
Built with arcade of moments!

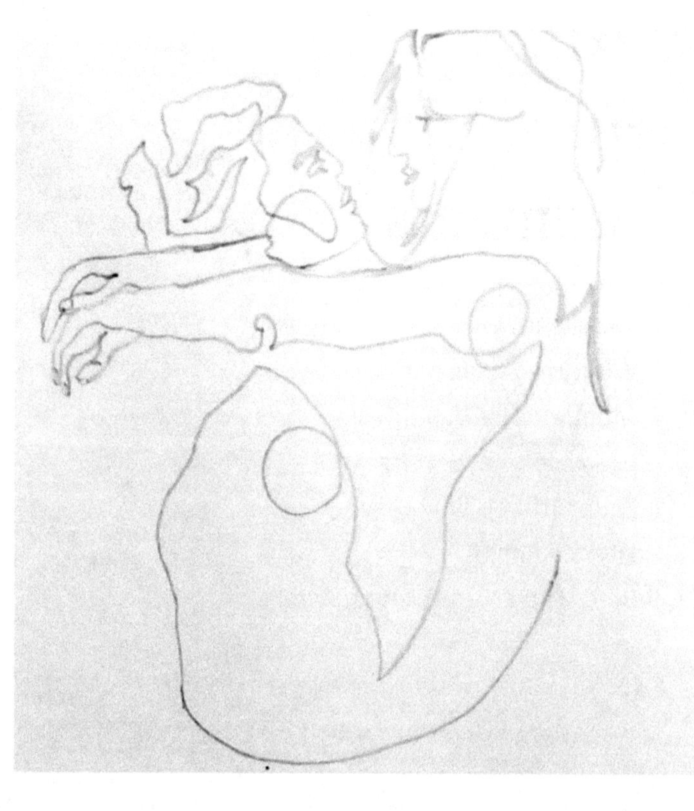

29. Sands of Love

We are trapped somewhere
within the sands of Love,
Our souls trapped in its grains.
I love you on its surface,
and I love you in its bed.
Whether its sunrise or sunset,
I love you even more yes!
This lifetime is not enough
to shower all that I have for you.
O dear! I can see you,
when I cannot see you!
For you are the melody
in my eyes.
They create you everywhere
for me to see,
with their own ink like a legacy.
Unaware of this felony sometimes,
I am confused if it's really you,
or the seas of my imagination?
And just like that,
I am trapped with you,
in this infinite time loop-
Flowing in the wind,
with sands of Love.

30. Home

I am clutter and chaos
and a rhyme of my own problems.
An unfinished painting,
whose painter is out and about
to find the new colors,
for painting this canvas.
But lost his way back somehow.
I do not wish to sort myself,
but wish to be sorted.
There are too many stars in the sky,
but their sparkle does not reach my eyes.
As they are blurred by the storms,
raging in me wild and high.
"I long for a home"-
Calls their scared silent cries.

They remain lost souls
like me tonight.
Too tired to find back their home,
which will again be taken away,
when the sun is up,
amidst the broad daylight.
So, for now,
with worries aside,

I wish to sleep here among stars.
At least they visit me every night.
In this unsaid promise, I am theirs,
and they are mine.

31. Falling for You

Yes, I feel weak in my knees
when you are around.
I am falling for you,
and there is no way around.
My emotions are at their peak,
and you are their prime.
But it is not owed to you,
Instead, a compliment
to the beauty of my mind.
O heartless soul, without a lover,
your existence is an illusion,
and your charm,
isn't worth a dime.

32. Sky in the Night

This sky in the night is so intimidating.
Sees me right into the eye.
Rips me and opens me apart,
Leaving me to wonder–
What is more attractive?
Its darkness or its mystery?
Oh! It is so beautiful,
That I cannot focus on its stars.
The wind is rushing
across my neck's shore,
while I gush to catch a breath.
It demands me to fly along,
When I can barely walk
Does it not know,
I am only a mere human
And not its fellow star?
But, am I not?
After all, we are all ashes
Walking hand in hand with time
Into the oblivion, little mimes.

33. Hostel Room

I think the safest place
for a girl is their hostel 'room'.
Safer than their parent's home,
safer than their husband's home.
It's something they don't have to share.
They are not just physically safe there,
their soul is safe too.
Safe enough to not
be subjected and suffocated,
to other's wishes and orders.

They are safe to choose,
If they want to go out and explore,
or be inside and devour.
They are safe to choose
their own chores,
and not be responsible for others.
These fellow comrades are
safe to hang out with friends.
They can choose anyone as
subject of their romance,
who they can choose
to be with in the future, or
move on as they personally grow.

Their choices do not cost them
their character castration.
These females are adorned with
the charm of independence, and
their freedom is their safety.
But to rest of us,
it costs us our chastity.

34. It will be over One Day

One day, I will wake up
and all of this will be over.
One day, these sufferings,
the agony, the restlessness
would be the things of past.

I will wake up as a fresh soul,
And that freshness,
will be strong enough
to protect itself.
But for now, I am torn!
I wonder why I am here
and when does it go?

Why do I have to be strong?
Is it not enough?
To be kind.
And why does everyone
strive to be strong?
Strength comes from suffering.
What do they get with this burning?
Or do they already know,

That suffering is inevitable?
So, putting up a fight
is the only solution.

I wonder when does it get over?
Or does it?
What if it keeps changing faces?
Never really leaving.
Finding new ways to strangle you
and crushing your battered soul
Until your death.

35. Wishes

I wish I did not have so many wishes.
Wish I did not have
such a wishful thinking,
for these wishes to come true.
I wish my wish dome
was a little empty.
For world is not a wish granting factory,
where wishes after wishes
are served as dishes of morning dew.

Even the wishes here wish
not to wish upon a wish,
that remains a wish.
I wish I did not have
these wishes that have
like a thousand wishers,
but not a single well-wisher!

36. Never Free!

Some dreams we will never be free of,
even if we keep our eyes wide open.
Some paths will never be ours,
even if we tread them strenuously.
Some faces will never be familiar,
even if we chase them endlessly.
So let go!
Let go before you are
too tired to stand back again.
Some renderings will never be enough
even if they are the best melodies.
So, choose your battles wisely.
The ones you have to fight
with the world,
and not yourself, because
some dreams will never be alive.
Yet some desires will never leave us alone.

37. Perhaps Because

My mother tells me
that I am too cynical,
likely for my own good.
Perhaps because I do not think
that love is beautiful,
that love will save us all,
and pull us away
when we get astray.
Perhaps because the only love
I have seen is the kind
that I do not deserve.
Perhaps because these days,
love is nothing but a text
left on read, which were written
when I was hungover.

My love is a stupid playlist
with their stupid names on it.
Perhaps because love these days,
is empty like our broken homes.
And when we meet the ones
with the beautiful indoors,
we lose control, and
try to build permanence,

in places, where we were
supposed to build tents.
Stupid! Stupid kids in love!
These days love is calculated
in terms of how much you give,
and how much you keep.
Meanwhile, I am horrible at
keeping track of things.
Maybe, I am the hollow one here
who cannot make them stay.
But sometimes,
I do get lost in museums,
and I hope you find me,
and you wish to stay, because
I might just be one stairwell away.

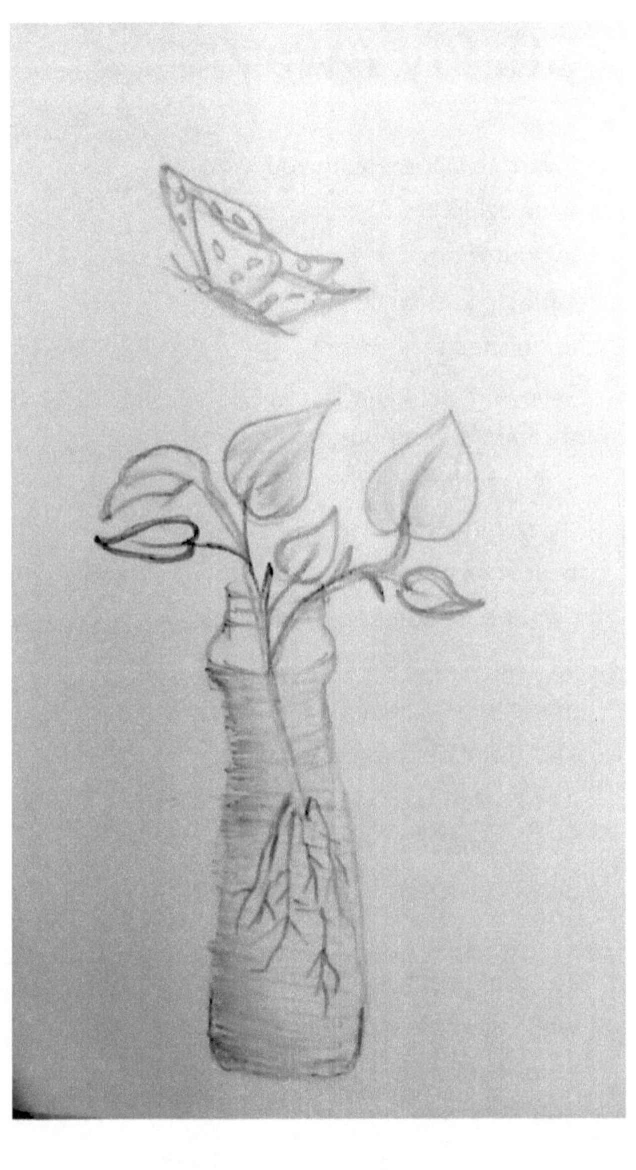

38. Fly Away

I want to sit here with you
once again.
In your room,
eating pizzas while we have
unfinished tasks to do.
Take late night strolls
through the campus,
or go randomly for
those random classes.
be it yoga or zumba.
I want to make these memories
all over again with you.
In the department, hostel,
and countless other places.
And I want to say to you-
That I want to lie here with you,
and share this moment with you.

You are quietly leaving,
while our past is flashing
before our eyes.
And we are surprised!
As if this was not supposed to happen.
Anyway, know that

while we go on with our lives,
we will always belong together.
In quite sighs, unsaid words,
unshared laughs and nostalgic gaze.
But for now, I just want to say
I want to lie here with you,
share some words, hugs, and laughs too.
through the night,
before the still silence catches on,
the morning comes,
and the stars are all gone.
And just like that, its dawn
the time for birds
to fly away from this lawn.

39. Convenience

People want to enjoy their rights,
but run away from responsibilities.
They will invest easily in new livings,
but cannot wait to
throw out the old beings.
This is the disease of humans-
seeking out new people constantly
and discarding the old ones completely.
And in keeping up with the new ones,
we keep changing.
So, in a while we are nothing
but empty vessels.

In clouds we wander.
With no grounds, we squander!
This wanderer chooses a big,
convenient ship to sail in life.
It avoids the small canoe
to not just remain alive,
but thrive.
But in this contempt,
of constantly changing clothes,
we peel off our skin,
and leave our pieces

in shards unkempt.
Until we finally lose ourselves,
inch by inch, among people
and become stories on bookshelves.
So, in the attempt to absolve ourselves,
we dissolve our-self.

40. Keep Going

Even in this stillness,
keep going!
Keep going, so that
this moment does not
become your finality.
Keep going,
just for the sake of it.
Keep going so that
you do not fall in this well,
and begin to rot.
Because time will not stop,
or turn to get you out.
Instead, it will leave you
with frogs of the well.
They will pull you down,
while you try to make out.
So, keep going!
Keep going, so that one day,
you get to recite your own story.
Instead, of the world to see
you as the sorry state of affairs.
A defected case seen with pity,
that nature chose to
throw out from its kitty.

41. Our Invisible World

I like it!
how our world between us
has a world of its own,
with a language of its own.
I like it!
how you touch me,
and with every touch,
you convey your feelings.
I keep saying that,
you do not share.
But you do,
with your touches.
When you are sad,
like a mommy,
I cuddle you to my chest.
And like a baby, you curl
slowly touching my breasts,
with heavy breathing and warm lips,
until you fall asleep.

I like it!
The heaviness in your breath,

and that you let them
out in my embrace.
I like it when you are angry,
you kiss me less and fume more,
let me move less and
bound me more.

I like it!
The way you show your pride in me.
Those days, you kiss me
on my forehead, instead of my neck.
You touch me a lot through your eyes,
and less with your pecks.
I like it!
When you are rejoiced.
Then you sway me round.
Like a toy you toss me around,
your kisses become pecks,
and in each other,
we find our ground.

42. Evolution

There are too many good things,
people and events in this world,
which we might never
meet or experience.
Such is the nature of nature.
It thrives on
the incompleteness of beings.
It moves forward through
the faded, lost love and its tragedy,
while we keep living in
compromises and half relations!
But such is the nature of nature.

To keep evolution moving,
there must be a missing link
To setup a goal.
We dream to reach there someday.
But it's only an apparition,
which thrives in us as a fantasy.
While trying to shape
our future in present,
our breaths keep dancing
in time lapses.
We slowly approach death,

while this illusion flourishes in us.
Our story ends,
But evolution progresses.

43. Nurtured

I hope you do not get
too many experiences,
to see the life and reality as it is.
I hope you are not
let down as much
to see things for what they are.

I hope you belong to
one of those blessed lot,
whose emotions are
well taken care of,
Whose perception of human connection,
and love is not constantly tarnished,
but nurtured and reciprocated.

44. Love, Acceptance and Validation

Love, acceptance,

Validation and the sense of belonging-

These are the tragedies of adulthood.

We constantly look for them,

when they are not there.

While we used to run around,

carefree in childhood,

when they were all there.

Adulting comes with life's harsh realities.

Strikes you hard in your gut,

exposing your helplessness in

your separation from your parents.

It tempts you into thinking

that you will better take care of them,

by being away from them.

It teaches you that time and distance

can erode you out of anyone's life.

Either it be the love of your life,

or your closest friends.

But time and distance are not

your complete enemies.

They also miraculously heal you,

and make you gradually
Learn to live again.
It's ironical, how you suddenly realise,
that selfish- a word and feeling
you always viewed in negative light,
suddenly becomes your savior.
Your care taker,
and just like that, at last,
you too learn to disappear
and move away.
As you fade from their world,
your visibility increases in your own.

45. This world is too big for me!

I realize that this world is too big
and I am very small.
There is no comparison.
I will be lost like a tiny ant!
And will never be enough for you.
You will mostly get more than,
what 1000s of me have for you.
But I have so much love for you,
like an ocean of unrequited feelings.
I do not know where to put them,
and who to give it to.
It's such a tragedy.
But this tragedy has been there for so long,
that I strive not to be sad about it,
Instead laugh and joke about it.
It is my stupid attempt to prevent
my stupid heart from being too broken.
Because I realise that
this world is too big for my story,
And doesn't care what goes on!

46. Trapped

When will I be free
of these dreams?
The dreams that hold me to you.
Inspite of thousands of
wounds and tears.
These dreams keep me trapped,
against my thousands of
well-weighed reasons.
They are worthless at the night,
a home to these irrational,
and stupid dreams about you!

47. A Lifetime ago

Sometimes I go back
to my younger self.
I don't mean time.
I mean life.
I live like I used to,
through sleepless nights,
and yawnful days.
Procrastinating and torturous ones!

The kind of low I feel,
reminds me the time
it has come from
to greet me.
It tells me how it was?
A lot of things, both good and bad.
It reminds me,
Why I put myself through it?
The tragic comedy of the situation
and most of all,
it reminds me
How I ended up here?
Then I come to realise,
that I might go there in flashes.
But I am never staying there.

Because I have moved on!
It now feels as if all that
existed a lifetime ago.

48. Present or Absent?

There are feelings that
I cannot express or write down.
But feel in me,
when I look at things or people,
smell a scent,
touch a feeling or a place.
These feelings slowly
take over me and
I am in their highs.
I do not know if
it's fragility of my heart
that I can't comprehend.

Or if it's the stupidity of my brain
that it can't really know their name.
When this happens, I am there,
but really absent.
Wandering somewhere else-
soul and mind!
These feelings sometimes,
strike me hard, or kiss me gently.

Sometimes they just pass by
like a breath of fresh air,
gently touching me by side.
Other times it's like a
Cold realisation or warmth of a new hope,
Or just a past memory playing on loop

Don't know if I do it,
Or it happens to me.
If, subconsciously I'm calling for it
or it just comes to me.
If its first,
I am a person of unkempt and
deep subconscious thoughts.
If its latter,
I am a person of weak and
unstable mind.
But doesn't it make me
lose myself from the present?
Because when I will have
flashes of 'the present' in my future,
I will have no clue
what was I doing there?
Because of my absence,

the imaginations again
will have a better hold of me.
Thus making me lost again,
absent even from my future.
Strewn chaotically in recalling
the feelings I never felt.
Yet they would touch me
in ways undefined and unexplained.

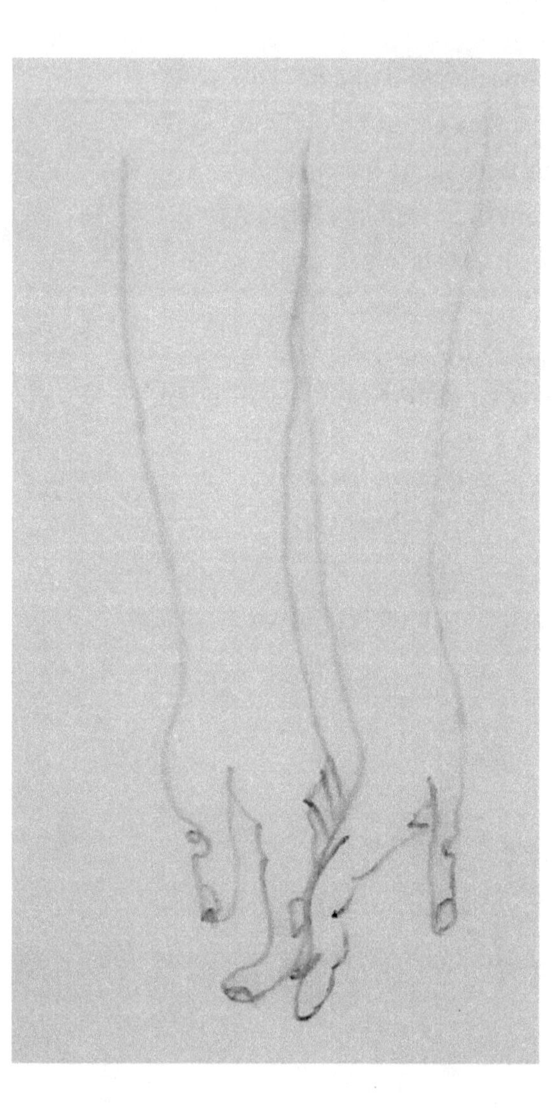

49. Wish I was there with you

I wish I was there with you,
when all the things
you were going through.
When you were at your most vulnerable,
and the situation was
not quite bendable!
I know you would
still make it without me!
And I am not someone,
you are looking out to see.
But I just want to be there for you,
take care of you,
like a shoulder for your
tired and vulnerable self.
Without disturbing you,
I would make things workable!
And not just in
your moments of pain,
but just in general.
I want to protect you
like a silent shield.
Diffuse the fatal blows

on your mind, body and soul.
Because I like that you exist.
I can see how it imparts
so many colors to this world.
So, I want to preserve YOU,
the most precious thing in the world.
Don't ask me why though?
Because I don't know myself.
It would require to
weigh my love for you.
And I am too fond of you
to question if it is true!
So, I offer you-
this affection as a tribute!

50. Ruins

We are all living in the ruins
of palaces of our dreams.
And our lives are the
novels which were never written.
But I still love you,
with each breath.
I would someday want to be
free from your curse,
and define life in my own verse.
As much as I know that
world does not care
How many hurts you endure?
or how many skies we kiss?
I live through it all for you!
Counting my blessings
to be beside you!

We are not made from money
and the world is not our oyster.
But you are my world, and beyond.
For me, the definition of love
is you!
I wish I could show you
how your name is etched

in my bones!
And I have an entirety of
memory bank saved for you.

51. Dearness to Dreadness

It is interesting how in time
the dearness of life,
changes into dreadness!
Because the flute can flute
but it cannot tambourine!

52. Maiden road

Beyond this balcony,
lies the great green forest.
And the road no one takes.
Like a maiden, it lays still.
Or maybe it is an old soul.
Reciting silent tales
of its old bustling days.
The ones that I cannot yet hear.
Because I have not yet
touched its soul.
But the time is running, and
I can feel it vibrating,
A throbbing of long-awaited calling.
Like it has waited for me a long time!
This makes me want to
go mingle with it and,
get away in its greens,
and not just look!

I want to feel myself in its mud,
like two lovers making love.
And rejoice at my new birth!
I want to feel it all,
on my skin and underneath.

The warmth of sun,
and the dread of wilderness.
Love has never been my escapade,
but it feels like reuniting
with a long-lost lover.
Revelling in the nectar
of its overflowing embrace.
The one who is touching me,
through its cool soothing breeze.
Tickling me with bird songs
and, I am losing myself
in the trance of its rustling leaves.

53. Feelings

How do I go back
when I have not gone ahead.
Take a step back,
when all that has moved
is my head.
It is pathetic to have one-sided
feelings for you.
I have no right
to obsess over you.
But believe me, it is no fun
to me either.
It's like a life-long mission
to have my heart listen.
and not wander with
the thoughts of you!
They ask what's so hard about it?
Honestly, I don't know myself.
Love is easy,
when expressed out loud!
Even with bare minimum words.
So tell me how do I
let go of something,
which was never on my side?

How do I spit out these emotions?
That I have to constantly
swallow and keep inside!

54. Irony

Why is it so?
That you want something,
but are extremely afraid of it.
Routinely, you are seeking it,
but overall running away from it.
You yearn to be understood,
but are afraid of being figured out,
keeping some parts of you hidden.
The more you reveal yourself,
makes you hide more parts of you.
The more you think about them,
makes you sicker and blue!
You are in the present,
without being present.
You are constantly depressed
while chasing happiness.
Laughing constantly throughout the day,
you are distraught by night.
Your emotions run so deep,
yet they make you
shallow from inside.
They are overflowing and overwhelming,
yet you are numb and empty inside.
In the quest of disappearing,

you yearn to be found.
While life within you is gradually dying,
you constantly wish that
it will be one-day worth living!

55. Greys

It was all white in the start,
in my first memory.
Then bits of it turned black,
turning it into
a pleasant pair of black and white.
But, as I grew,
the world started to dilate.
And those places were taken by
different shades of- grey.
Grey- a color not too black,
and not too white.
But a melody in blend
of black and white.
This unison of perfection, ironically
sets their fight in motion.
With both trying to dominate,
we all become different shades of grey.
These greys keep changing over time.
A reflection of our persona perhaps.
With constant changing sides
of black and white,
our world became an
inhabitation of greys.
These greys brought us together,

and set us apart.
But, despite these differences,
our lives are a way back to each other.
While our greys deceive us,
unknowingly we gravitate towards
each other,
embracing our incompleteness.
This is the recipe to our completeness,
our blacks and whites-
a canvas holding us all together.